CONTENTS

KU-260-882

Some words are shown in bold, **like this**.
You can find out what they mean by looking in the glossary.

WHAT IS PREHISTORIC ART?

Put simply, prehistoric people were people who did not have writing. Different groups of people left the prehistoric period at different times when they started to use writing. Prehistoric art was art made during this period. Some people still have no writing. They live today as their **ancestors** did. The art they make today is still called prehistoric art.

The development of writing was different all over the world. The earliest writing we know about was invented in Sumeria around 3250 BC. This first writing was little pictures, or **pictograms**, not alphabets like the one we use. Soon people began using **stylized** picture symbols to write about themselves and what they did. These help us to study history.

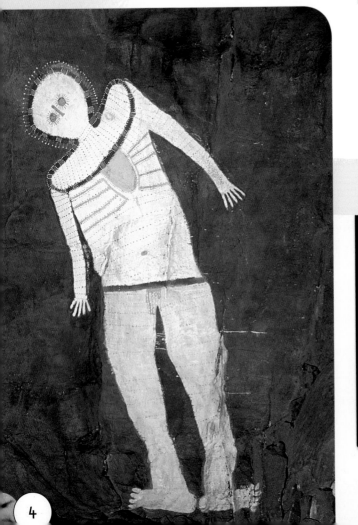

Wandjina Rain Spirit, Kimberley, in Western Australia, rock painting

Australian Aboriginals are made up of over 750 tribal groups. White Wandjina spirits like this were painted thousands of years ago on rock surfaces, in the Kimberley region of Western Australia. Wandjina spirits are very powerful spirit-beings, recognized by some Aboriginal groups of this region as being responsible for storms and rain. Clouds encircle the spirit's head like a halo. It has no mouth or ears.

Prehistoric Art

Susie Hodge

www.heinemann.co.uk/library
Visit our website to find out more information about Heinemann Library books.

To order:
☎ Phone 44 (0) 1865 888112
📄 Send a fax to 44 (0) 1865 314091
💻 Visit the Heinemann bookshop at www.heinemann.co.uk/library to browse our catalogue and order online.

First published in Great Britain by Heinemann Library, Halley Court, Jordan Hill, Oxford OX2 8EJ, part of Harcourt Education.

Heinemann is a registered trademark of Harcourt Education Ltd.

Editorial: Clare Lewis
Design: Victoria Bevan, Michelle Lisseter, and Q2A Media
Illustrations: Oxford Illustrators
Picture Research: Erica Newbery
Production: Helen McCreath

Printed in China

ISBN 978 0 431 05674 6 (hardback)
10 09 08 07 06
10 9 8 7 6 5 4 3 2 1

ISBN 978 0 431 05806 1 (paperback)
11 10 09 08 07
10 9 8 7 6 5 4 3 2 1

British Library Cataloguing in Publication Data
Hodge, Susie
Art in History: Prehistoric Art – 2nd edition
709.4'1'09031
A full catalogue record for this book is available from the British Library.

Acknowledgements
The publishers would like to thank the following for permission to reproduce photographs:
Ancient Art & Architecture Collection, M. Andrews p.**29** (right), R. Sheridan pp.**12**, **14**, **16**, **17**, **20**, **22**; Count Robert Bégoüen, Musée Pujol, Paris p.**29** (left); The Bridgeman Art Library p.**15**; Colorphoto Hinz Allschwil-Basel pp.**6**, **10**, **13**; Corbis, W. Kaehler p.**21**, A. Woolfitt p.**5**; C. M. Dixon pp.**7**, **8**, **19**; Fortean Picture Library, D. Stacy p.**28**; Lauros Giraudon, Paris p.**18**; Robert Harding Picture Library, F. Jackson p.**24**, Larsen-Collinge Int. p.**4**; Werner Forman Archive, Anthropology Museum, Veracruz University, Jalapa p.**26**, Auckland Institute & Museum, Auckland p.**23**, British Museum p.**25**, Field Museum of Natural History, Chicago p.**27**

Cover picture of hand paintings, South America, reproduced with permission of The Art Archive/ Dagli Orti.

Every effort has been made to contact copyright holders of any material reproduced in this book. Any omissions will be rectified in subsequent printings if notice is given to the publishers.

The paper used to print this book comes from sustainable resources.

This is one of the most striking ancient monuments still standing. Huge stones were placed upright in a circle, with others laid on top of them. It was made by European **Neolithic** people and is known as a **megalith**. Megaliths were used as tombs or for religious purposes.

The first art

There have been humans on Earth for more than 4 million years. But we have no record of art before about 35,000 years ago. We know little about the first artists, but we can find clues in the art itself. Most art seems to have been made for special purposes or was to do with certain beliefs.

Timechart	Europe	Middle East	Africa	Asia	The Americas	Australasia
BC	Paleolithic period					Rock art
35,000						
25,000	Venus statues					
15,000	Relief sculpture				Cave Art - Brazil	
10,000	Mesolithic period	E N D	O F	I C E	A G E	
8000	Neolithic period		Rock Art - Sahara	Pottery - China		
4000	Rock painting & pottery					Aborigine bark paintings and carvings
3500		Summerians and Egypptians developed writing – pictograms				
2000	Megaliths Mycenaean civilization - Greece		Sahara begins to dry out			
1000		Iron first used			Olmec sculpture	
AD						
150						
700						Polynesian tribal art Maori art in New Zealand
800					Tribal art - sand painting, totem art	
1000			Ife Kingdom sculptures			

IDEAS AND MEANINGS

Because prehistoric people had no writing, they did not leave us records about what they thought or did. So to find out about their thoughts about art we have to look for evidence in the art itself.

Magic art

One of the first and most important reasons why people created images seems to be because they believed art was a form of magic. They believed art could protect them against other powers, such as the forces of nature or unearthly gods. Some art was made to ask the spirits for success in hunting or for the birth of babies.

This was painted on the walls of an underground cave. Many similar paintings have been discovered in caves in other parts of France and in Spain. Some people believe these paintings were made to help hunters catch their prey in a magical way.

Galloping Horse, Lascaux in France, c. 13,000 BC,
Paleolithic, *1.4m (4ft 7in), cave painting*

Clues and evidence

Artists took great trouble in making their pictures. Several clues help solve the mystery of why they were painted. Many are of hunting scenes. Sometimes an animal's insides, such as the heart, are drawn outside the animal. Perhaps this was to show which parts the hunter should aim to hit.

More importantly, pictures were often painted on top of each other. Some are almost completely covered with other paintings. This may show that the paintings were meant to be more than just beautiful pictures.

Perhaps if some wall paintings were thought to have made a hunt successful, then that piece of wall may have been seen as lucky. People would then have wanted to use the same piece of wall again for more paintings.

Many footprints have been found on the hardened clay floor in front of the pictures. Perhaps people danced there, in a kind of ceremony. Similar clues about prehistoric art have been discovered in other parts of the world.

Horseman of the Altai, Pazyryk in Siberia, c. 400 BC, Neolithic, felt

This felt wall-hanging was preserved by the frozen surroundings. It shows how riders dressed, the weapons they carried, the fashion for fancy moustaches, and how skilful the artists were.

MATERIALS AND METHODS

Prehistoric artists probably spent years learning and practising their craft. Many sketches and corrected drawings have been found alongside other surviving prehistoric pictures. This may be evidence that skilled, older artists taught younger ones.

Hand prints

Some of the earliest images that have been found were made by families. They are hand prints. Adults and children placed their hands against a greased wall and blew **pigment** through hollow sticks over them. When they took their hands away, the hand shape was left.

Finger painting

Early artists created skilful and realistic images. Pictures of animals found in caves were produced using the most basic tools and equipment. We think that artists applied paint by blowing through hollow sticks or bones. They also used leather pads, feathers, fur, sticks with the ends crunched (or chewed) into a kind of brush, or their fingers.

Can you see the hand print above the spotted horse? Hands were used as stencils pressed against the rock and colour was blown over them. Colour-stained bone tubes have been found that held the powder. Hands were powerful symbols in prehistoric times. They could use tools and utensils. They could also make things and signal to other people.

Hand prints, Pech Merle in France, c. 18,000 BC, Paleolithic, cave painting print

The Great Serpent Mound, Ohio in USA, 100 BC – AD 500, approximately 450m (1,476ft) long, earthwork

Some artworks were not made with paint at all. This huge snake-like mound was built by the Adena people. It is thought to be a religious monument, as it can only be seen clearly from above. Imagining what it would look like, artists heaped soil into the serpent shape. Other animal-shaped mounds were made in the same way.

How paints were made

Paints were made by crushing **minerals** into powder and putting them onto damp surfaces, such as rock. Sometimes the powder was mixed with wax or oil to make it stick to other surfaces, such as hide, wood, or bone. Powdered pigments were kept in hollow bone tubes.

Crushed rocks and earth produced browns, yellows, reds, and oranges. Powdered **charcoal** gave black; another rock, called manganese, produced violet; chalk made white. Greens and blues came from crushed rocks, but these rocks were not found everywhere in the world.

THE FIRST ARTISTS

The oldest art we know about was made by the people of the Paleolithic or Old Stone Age period (from about 35,000 BC to 10,000 BC). This was during the last Ice Age which lasted for thousands of years and was actually several alternate cold and warm periods. The art includes cave paintings, hand prints, and small statues.

Lifelike pictures

Paleolithic cave paintings were first discovered in France and Spain, although similar paintings have since been found in other parts of the world. At first, **archaeologists** did not believe that such skilful pictures could have been created by primitive people. But they changed their minds when rough stone and bone tools used by the Paleolithic artists were found near by.

The Hall of Bulls, Lascaux in France, c. 12,000 BC, Paleolithic, largest bull is 5.5m (18ft) long, cave painting

Paintings of bulls cover the walls and roof of this cave. Most of them were painted showing a side view and are larger than lifesize. They were painted carefully so each bull is in **proportion**. They seem to stampede over the walls. Smaller outlines of deer run in between.

Make your own cave painting

Materials:

- **sheet of card**
- **paper**
- **paste**
- **grey paint**
- **coloured chalk**
- **twigs**

1. Tear paper into small pieces and scrunch it up. Paste it to the card and cover it with more paste.

2. Paste on a top layer of torn but smooth paper. Let it dry, then paint it grey. Now you have a cave as wall.

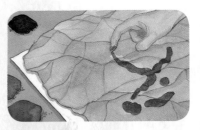

3. When this is dry, crush the chalks and use twigs or your fingers to paint a picture.

Hunting pictures

Paleolithic artists painted the animals they hunted, such as bulls, bison, or mammoths. Many experts think that the artists believed they captured the animal's soul when they painted it. This could be why the images are so lifelike – if the artists captured the animal's true likeness, they would be sure to capture the real thing during the hunt.

Whatever the paintings meant, surely no one would have crawled so deep into these caves to paint unless the pictures had a serious meaning. Dark and eerie, the caves were probably sacred places for Paleolithic people and the art was part of their beliefs.

THE POWER OF PAINTING

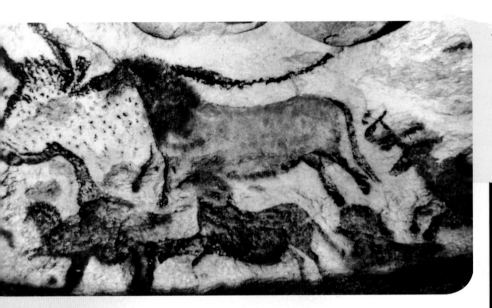

*This large bull is jumping over a **frieze** of little horses. Notice how **shading** helps to make the bull seem lifelike, solid, and strong.*

The earliest people spent most of their lives hunting animals and gathering wild fruits. Getting enough food to eat could be a problem. Artists were probably considered to have special powers. People thought their art would help make hunting successful.

Magical cave paintings

These paintings of animals were made deep inside caves in France, Spain, Africa, North America, and Australia. The caves were far away from where people lived. Artists and tribes seemed to believe that they gained magical powers over animals by painting them. Some paintings had arrows and spears painted on them or were actually shot at with real weapons after the painting was finished. Perhaps the people thought this would help the hunters catch their prey. By painting more animals, perhaps they thought they could increase the size of the herds.

Most of the paintings are as large as, or larger than, life. They must have seemed powerful and unearthly on the rough walls.

The Dead Man, Lascaux in France, c. 16,000 BC, Paleolithic, cave painting

Evil spirits

Many objects and paintings used for different types of magic have been found around the world. They come from different prehistoric societies. Some of this art was used to cure illnesses or to ward off evil spirits.

How artists worked in the dark

To paint pictures in dark caves, artists made lamps from large hollow stones, seashells, or bowls made from skulls. They filled them with animal fat, then added locks of hair, fur, or pieces of dried moss to use as wicks and set them alight.

This painting seems to have a powerful meaning. The bird-headed man has been killed by the bison. The bird on the stick is thought to be the man's spirit. The bison has been killed by a giant spear, but a rhinoceros is escaping unharmed. It seems unlikely that cave paintings like this were for decoration, as many pictures were painted on top of others. Perhaps once a picture had served its special purpose, it was believed to lose its magical powers.

PEOPLE IN PICTURES

Since the first hand prints on cave walls in about 18,000 BC, people have wanted to produce images of themselves. The earliest artists painted stick figures alongside realistic-looking wild animals. Perhaps the human figures were unrealistic because they believed that accurate images stole a person's or animal's soul and they were afraid of taking a person's soul.

A change of art

About 10,000 years ago, a warmer climate caused huge forests to cover some of the plains where people had hunted. The warmer climate meant that larger animals could not survive. It appears that at the same time cave art was no longer needed. People moved to areas where they could farm and breed animals. Their lifestyles were more settled and they had extra time to create art. Art seems to have been used more for decoration than it had before. **Mesolithic** (Middle Stone Age) and Neolithic (New Stone Age) artists began painting on open rock surfaces instead of in dark caves. They included more people in their pictures.

Battle Scene, Valltorta in Spain, c. 9000 BC, Mesolithic, length 2.9m (9ft 6in), rock painting

These lively little Mesolithic figures are stylized and entirely different from the earlier realistic-looking Paleolithic cave animals. Painted on rock walls, they form a pattern of curves and angles. **Composition**, or layout, was something new that artists were beginning to consider.

People from Jabbaren, Algeria in Africa, 6000– 1000 BC, Neolithic, cave painting

These people are painted simply, with only one pigment. Yet you can see clearly that they are African tribespeople, possibly from one family. Several paintings from this area show us that what is now desert, was once fertile farmland.

Caricatures

As you can see from the battle scene on page 14, some figures from this period look quite frightening even though they do not look realistic. Some parts of their bodies are exaggerated and some parts are lessened. They are **caricatures** of humans.

Prehistoric artists from different societies created caricatures when making human images. Ancient tribes from Papua New Guinea made face masks by painting simple, **geometric** shapes in the right places. They painted a triangle for the nose, circles for the eyes, and so on. Native Americans carved faces on top of each other on totem poles, sometimes including just one or two recognizable features.

PREHISTORIC POTTERY

Prehistoric people used pots to store things and to eat out of. At first they made them out of all sorts of materials, including tree bark, leather, bone, and stone. Then about 10,000 years ago people started to make pottery.

Making pots

First, the clay was dug from the ground. It was mixed with something dry, such as sand, shells, or powdered plants, to make it firm.

It was then rolled and kneaded to make it soft enough to shape. Small containers were easy to make from one piece of clay. Larger vessels were often built up with several strips or coils.

Artists discovered that the clay hardened and became stronger when it was heated. After each pot had been **fired (**heated in a fire or oven**)**, it was taken out and smoothed one last time to make sure there were no holes. Many early pots were engraved as well as painted. Once the pots had been fired, they could be used to eat or drink from, or to store things in, such as grain. Clay pots were particularly important before metals were discovered.

Urn of Garisu, Kansu in China, c. 2500 BC, Neolithic, clay

This jar has been made with one of the earliest **potter's wheels**. By using the wheel, the surface was made smooth and even. The patterns would have been painted on the pot before the clay had dried.

Beaker people

Although prehistoric tools were simple, the craftwork produced was beautiful. The Beaker people are named after the beaker-like pots that have been found in early Bronze Age graves in Europe. This attractive pottery was made without the help of a potter's wheel. They had delicate patterns stamped on them in the same way as we print patterns today.

Decorated vessel, Bulgaria in Europe, 6000–5800 BC, Neolithic, clay

The people who made these vessels lived in wooden framed houses in villages in Bulgaria. They often shaped their pots like animals. The surface patterns were popular in the area at that time.

RELIEF CARVING

Relief carving is a mix of drawing and sculpture. Relief pictures are raised from the surface. To make them, artists have to be able to draw, carve, and use different tools. Prehistoric relief pictures were made in rock, stone, bone, horn, and wood.

Carved caves

In southern France and Spain in about 19,000 BC, rock faces were carved with friezes of animals (cows, bison, ibex, deer, birds, and even badgers).

Artists used the natural lumps and bumps of the rock surfaces to create animals' shoulders or backs. In the flickering light of prehistoric lamps these carved animal pictures must have appeared to move around the shadowy caves. Other similar cave carvings have been found elsewhere in Europe, often in the darkest depths of caves. Later carvings have been found on open-air rock surfaces or in shallow caves in Eastern Europe.

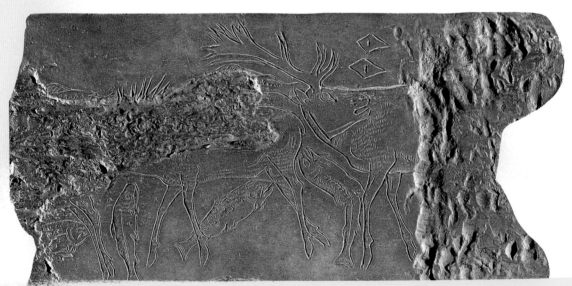

Stags and Salmon Engraving, Lortet in France, c. 15,000 BC, Paleolithic, stone

This engraving shows a stag looking backwards – an unusual and difficult angle and a change from the flat, sideways-on view that most paintings showed. You can also see how artists were making marks to show light and shade and fur and scales.

Bison Spear-thrower, Dordogne in France, c. 12,000 BC, Paleolithic, reindeer antler

From carving to engraving

Most relief carving was done between 21,000 and 12,000 BC. Afterwards, **engraving** was used more often. Engraving means carving inwardly, rather than making raised images. As engraving became more common, so too did stylized patterns and pictures. Carving became less lifelike and more geometric.

This carving on a reindeer antler was found in a cave called La Madeleine in the south of France. The antler was used for holding and throwing spears. It is quite lifelike and has turned its head to lick its side.

Good luck charms

Bones and antlers were carved with pictures of animals, such as bison, mammoths, wild horses, or deer. Some show humans following the animals. These carvings may have been used as good luck charms and carried on hunts.

STATUES AND SCULPTURE

Some of the most mysterious pieces of prehistoric art are fat little female statues with no faces. They have been named Venus figurines. More than 60 Venus figurines have been found throughout Europe, from Spain to Russia. They date from around 25,000 to 15,000 BC.

Venus Figurine, Willendorf in Austria, c. 25,000 BC, Paleolithic, 11.5cm (4.5in), limestone

This is the best known of the Venus figurines. She was once painted red. Some traces of the paint remain. Perhaps people believed that these fat or pregnant women were mother-goddesses who helped women have babies.

The Bronze Age

Prehistoric sculptors became highly skilled in using all kinds of local materials. These depended on where they lived, but included stone, bone, shell, horn, bark, or wood. Many also modelled in clay. When metals were discovered in about 4000 BC, many sculptors worked in copper and **bronze**. Bronze was easier to work with than stone and better than any other material then known. Its use spread across the world, giving its name to the Bronze Age.

Wrong proportions

Some **terracotta** heads were found in Africa. They were made in about 300 BC. They are the same size as real heads, with detailed eyes, nose, mouth, and complicated hairstyles. Some were attached to much smaller bodies. We do not know exactly what they were for or why they were out of proportion to their bodies. But we do know that they were believed to please the spirits.

These enormous human-like statues guard Easter Island in the Pacific. The eyes were made of white coral. Tattoos were painted on the bodies. Nobody today knows why they were made or who made them. They do not appear to represent real people, but they are human-shaped. They seem to guard the island, or perhaps they are looking out to sea for something.

Guardian Figures, Easter Island,
c. AD 1000, 4–5m (13–16ft) high, rock

PACIFIC ART

Many different groups of people lived around the Pacific Ocean, from the Aboriginal people in Australia to the Polynesians. The Polynesians spread south to New Zealand, from Hawaii in the north and Easter Island in the east. Most early islanders lived in tribes, hunting, farming, and fishing. Most Pacific tribes honoured the spirits of their ancestors, believing that they had the power to bring good or bad luck. The Pacific peoples had different styles and different ideas of beauty. Some Pacific art was realistic and some was stylized.

Aboriginal art

For thousands of years the art of the Australian Aboriginals has been an important part of their lives. It includes bark and rock paintings, rock carvings, shell engravings, and wooden sculptures. Aboriginals decorated many of the objects they used in everyday life, such as spears, boomerangs, and baskets. Today they believe that art should not be locked up in museums.

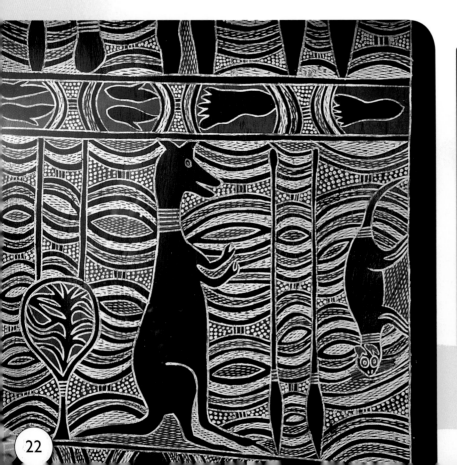

Dreamings relate to creation times in Aboriginal religious tradition. This picture tells us about the creative activity of one of the great creature-beings who took the form of a kangaroo. The painting describes a section of the kangaroo's journey through one Aboriginal group's land. Footprints always represent a journey in this kind of art.

Kangaroo Dreaming, Australia 1989, synthetic polymer on canvas

Maori Carved Head, Waitangi in New Zealand, c. AD 800, wood carving with inlaid shell eyes

This head represents a Maori ancestor who would have been recognized by his distinctive pattern of facial tattoos. To the Maori, facial tattoos were a sign of great courage and revealed a person's true personality.

Amazing skills

Many Pacific artists developed amazing skills. Considering the simple tools they used, much of their detailed work was astonishing. In New Zealand, Maori woodcarving is extremely complicated and is still made today. As well as being complicated or detailed, much of this art also shows great freedom of imagination and expression. Each tribe had their own style, but individual artists had their own interpretations. Artists knew that they were producing art that was meant to last, even when it was made for a single festive occasion.

AFRICAN ART

Africa stretches across more than 30 million square kilometres (11.5 million square miles). It is said to be the birthplace of the human race and some of the earliest art has been found there. There were many different tribes in Africa who did not know that other tribes existed. The first works of art produced there were paintings and engravings in the Sahara before it was a desert, in about 7000 BC. Pictures have been found on rock surfaces that seem to be about ancient tribal beliefs.

Art for the spirits
Like the art of the Pacific regions, it seems that much African art was made to please the spirits. The art of different tribes shows that they believed in different spirits and traditions.

Some of the finest African art was sculpture. This included masks and statues made from wood, ivory, stone, terracotta, raffia, mud, and, later, iron and bronze. Artists carved statuettes that were probably thought to have healing and protecting powers.

This rock painting of copper-coloured men farming, comes from the Sahara region in Africa. It shows us that the Sahara was once fertile and how the people farmed. All the mountainous regions of the Sahara contain rock paintings.

Herdsman and Cattle, Tassili in Algeria, c. 6500 BC, Neolithic, figures between 1.5–3.5m (4–12ft) high, rock painting

Bronze figure, Ife in West Africa, c. AD 1200, 4.6m (15ft), bronze

This statue may be of a king. Advanced **techniques** have been used to make it (the process was later lost). Perhaps these skilled artists learned their techniques from other more advanced tribes who moved into the area. Similar terracotta sculptures were found less than 30 km (18 miles) away. They were possibly made by other tribes but we do not know for sure.

Tribal traditions

Artists were probably **commissioned** to work by chieftains, heads of families, and other important people. In some tribes, the job of artist was often passed from father to son. Training probably lasted for many years. Artists had to learn the traditions of both the art and religion of their tribe. Some tribal art involved music and dancing as well as decorative carvings, statues, and masks.

AMERICAN ART

As in Africa, American tribes grew up far away from each other. Each tribe developed its own beliefs and colourful art.

Central American art

About 32,000 years ago, Stone Age hunters arrived in North America and travelled south to Mexico. Gradually several civilizations developed. The Olmecs, in southern Mexico, developed building methods and designed picture-signs which experts are only just beginning to understand. They carved huge stone heads, some up to 3 metres (10 feet) high. These are probably **portraits** of their most important people.

Olmec Colossal Head, Mexico, c. 1500–300 BC, Mesolithic to Neolithic, 3m (10ft), stone

This stone head is one of 16 that is believed to have been made by the Olmec civilization. They each weigh about 10 tonnes. We are not sure if they are the heads of gods or rulers, but they all have similar faces and wear circular helmets.

Copper Bird, Ohio in North America, c. 100 BC, Neolithic, 38cm (1ft 3in), copper and pearl

This bird, which is a raven or a crow, was made by an artist from the Ohio river valley. Several more sculptures of animals have been found nearby. Although the artist used few materials and worked with simple tools, the bird is quite detailed.

North America

Some of the hunters who came from Asia into North America spread across the United States and Canada and formed different tribal groups.

Native American peoples such as the Inuits from the Arctic regions, the Sioux from the Great Plains, and the various pueblo-dwellers of the south-west, are the descendants of these early Stone Age hunters.

The early North Americans left behind objects that we use today to identify the many different tribes, such as pottery, tools, weapons, sculptures, carvings, animal-shaped mounds, and sand pictures.

South America

Groups of peoples also spread throughout Central and South America. The earliest civilization in South America seems to have been the Chavin, who lived in the Andes Mountains from about 1250 BC to 200 BC. They made pottery, tools, weapons, sculptures, and carvings.

There are many other Central and South American tribal groups, each with their own types of art. We can identify how different groups lived by examining the types of art they left behind.

UNDERSTANDING PREHISTORIC ART

Inventive art

Prehistoric art shows us clearly how art changes as people's lifestyles change. It also shows that the most realistic art is not necessarily the most skilful. Sometimes the ideas and imagination behind the art are more important than the technical skills. The first prehistoric artists had to rely more on their natural skills than later artists who developed better tools and equipment. This shows us how inventive artists can be.

How styles developed

By the end of the Paleolithic period, artists had developed three styles. Art has changed since then. But even now it usually follows one of these first three styles.

1. Natural art
(a realistic-looking, recognizable copy of something)

Jade figure, Mexico, c. 400 BC, Neolithic, jade

Although the Olmec people (about 1250 to 400 BC) had only Stone Age tools, they were gifted sculptors. This statue is made from a semi-precious green stone called **jade** and is probably a likeness of one of their kings or gods. We do not know who he was, but we can see it is an accurate and recognizable description of a man.

2. Picture signs

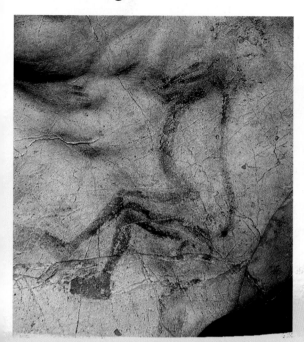

Sorcerer, Trois Frères in France, c. 15,000 BC, Paleolithic, 75cm (2ft 5in) high, cave painting

This painting, known as the Sorcerer, was found on the wall of a cave in France. It shows a man with antlers on his head who may have been taking part in a **ritual** dance. Perhaps he is asking the spirits for a successful hunt. It is not a realistic representation but it is a simple description that could be understood by others.

3. Decorative artpatterns

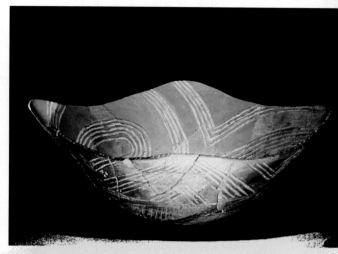

Patterned pot, Romania, c. 4000 BC, Neolithic, height 13.7cm (5in), clay

Swirls, spirals, circles, and zigzags became popular pottery decorations during the Stone Age. Archaeologists can sometimes tell where a pot was made by looking at its pattern. Geometric patterns were used after lifelike cave art became less important and people had more time to create art.

Primitive pictures

Primitive art is different to prehistoric art. Primitive art is usually based on a simple view of what the artist knew to be there. It was not based on a careful look at an object.

Some prehistoric artists made primitive art, but they were also skilled at non-primitive art such as realistic animal paintings and statues. Which kind of art do you prefer?

TIMELINE

BC

35,000   Upper Paleolithic Period (Later Old Stone Age). The first hand prints and cave paintings are made in Europe.

30,000   Asian people arrive in North America.

25,000   Venus of Willendorf is carved. Small sculptures are made of stone, horn, mammoth ivory, and bone.

15,000   Relief sculpture of animals are made in caves in France and Spain. Cave paintings continue. Hunters move to Mexico.

10,000   Mesolithic Age (Middle Stone Age). The Ice Age ends. Tools, farming, and breeding animals are improved. Painting is done on rock walls.

8500   The first rock art is made in the Sahara region.

8000   Neolithic Age (New Stone Age). Most big game animals die out.

4000   Aboriginal people make rock and bark paintings in Australia. Inuit people produce carvings in the Arctic.

3600   Egyptians settle around the River Nile. Sumerians develop writing, and later the Egyptians do too. This puts them out of the prehistoric period.

3000   Islanders around the Pacific Ocean produce carvings and other art.

2000   Stonehenge is built in Britain.

1500–300   Olmec people make carvings in Mexico, including colossal stone heads.

400   Felt wall-hangings are made in Siberia.

300   Celtic art appears in Britain.

100   Mayan culture develops in Mexico. Hieroglyphs are developed which puts these people out of the prehistoric period.

   The Great Serpent Mound and copper carvings are created in North America.

AD

750   Maoris from Polynesia settle in New Zealand.

1000   Enormous Easter Island statues are carved

1100   The Ife Kingdom develops in West Africa. Bronzes and carvings are created.

GLOSSARY

ancestor member of the same family who lived long ago

archaeologist person who studies the past by looking at old remains and objects

bronze hard-wearing, brownish-gold metal, a mixture of copper and tin

caricature picture or imitation of a person that exaggerates certain features

charcoal black material that is left when wood or bones are burned

commissioned ordered and paid for

composition layout, or arrangement, of art

engraving carved lines, making pictures or patterns

fired heated or baked

frieze band or strip of decoration

geometric with lines, angles, and shapes, such as squares, triangles, and circles

jade a hard stone, usually green and especially popular in the Far East

megalith large monument made of stones or boulders

Mesolithic time between about 10,000 BC and 8000 BC

mineral natural rock or stone

Neolithic New Stone Age – time between about 8000 BC and 5000 BC

Paleolithic Old Stone Age – time from before 35,000 BC until about 10,000 BC

pictogram little picture used as a symbol to mean something

pigment coloured powder made from plants, minerals, or animals and mixed with various liquids to make paint

portrait image of a particular person

potter's wheel circle of wood or stone that was spun around when wet clay was on it, so that the sides of a pot could be smoothed easily

proportion correct size of things in relation to each other

relief raised carved picture

ritual ceremony

shade to add deeper colour in darker areas

stylized designed and usually made simpler, but also decorative

technique way of working

terracotta means "baked earth". It is clay, usually a reddish-brown and is used to make pottery and statues.

FIND OUT MORE

You can find out more about prehistoric art in books and on the Internet. Use a search engine such as www.yahooligans.com to search for information. A search for the words "prehistoric art" will bring back lots of results, but it may be difficult to find the information you want. Try refining your search to look for some of the people and ideas mentioned in this book, such as "Maoris" or "cave paintings".

More books to read

Wood, Robert M. *How it Works: Discovering Prehistory*. London: Horus Editions, 2002.
Eyewitness Books: *Early Humans*. London, Dorling Kindersley, 2005

INDEX

Numbers in plain type (24) refer to the text.

Numbers in bold type (**28**) refer to an illustration.